THE ITTY BITTY GUIDE TO

tipping

about the authors

Stacie Krajchir works as a television producer and lives in Venice Beach, California.

Carrie Rosten is a wardrobe stylist and costume designer. She lives in Los Angeles, California.

They are the co-founders of The Bungalow, a creative services agency specializing in publicity, event planning, and promotions.

ALSO AVAILABLE

Other books in the Itty Bitty *series include:*

The Itty Bitty Guide to Business Travel

THE ITTY BITTY GUIDE TO

tipping

BY STACIE KRAJCHIR
AND CARRIE ROSTEN

CHRONICLE BOOKS
SAN FRANCISCO

Text copyright © 2004 by Stacie Krajchir and Carrie Rosten.
All rights reserved. No part of this book may be reproduced in
any form without written permission from the publisher.

Library of Congress Cataloging-in-Publication Data available.

ISBN: 0-8118-4038-7

Manufactured in China

Designed by Ayako Akazawa

Distributed in Canada by Raincoast Books

9050 Shaughnessy Street

Vancouver, British Columbia V6P 6E5

10 9 8 7 6 5 4 3 2 1

Chronicle Books LLC

85 Second Street

San Francisco, California 94105

www.chroniclebooks.com

To all of our former customers, managers, and coworkers at the Pier Market, who, through the good, the bad, and the ugly inspired this book. To all those in the industry who allowed us to ask questions, do interviews, and call back just "one more time"— thank you for your contributions. A special thanks to Craddock, Jen Summers, Yifat Oren, Angelina Umansky, Nickie, and Denny. Grateful thanks to our legal leader and dear friend Nikki Harvat, for her insight and tenacity, for guiding us on this maiden voyage, and for her continued support of our creative ventures. To Anne Bunn for trusting her instinct that tipping was a great idea—and for giving us a clear, detailed introduction to the publishing world. To our guiding light and creative spearhead at Chronicle Books, our editor extraordinaire Mikyla Bruder, who truly taught us what making a book was all about, and helped keep our vision alive every step of the way. Thank you for believing in the Itty Bitty series. Thanks to Leslie Davisson, our sassy behind-the-scenes copilot at Chronicle who took on and walked us through so many details, thank you for keeping us on track and getting us to the station! To our wonderful friends and families who continuously support us in so many ways, from listening to us talk endlessly about tipping to understanding when we couldn't make a function because we were on deadline. Thank you for being there for us and inspiring us always, especially Clarene, Alex, Sue, Nana, Papa, Richard, Carol, Nickie, Denny, Phin, Pam, Andres, Maxwell, Princess, Andy, and our family at Extra. Last but definitely not least, to the service industry folks, who endure day after day of getting stiffed, hearing complaints, repeating the list of salad dressings and beers available, serving water with lemon, dealing with substitutions and separate checks, being called "sweetie" and "honey," and being asked what their real job is—this is no itty bitty task—and we know that you are the true heroes. THANK YOU!

Tipping dedication:
To the original chowder slingin' crew: Joao, Guyo, Jack, Tony, and DJ— our biggest "tip" then, now and always.

contents

introduction

Let's face it: tipping can be confusing, embarrassing, and awkward. Whether you want to convey your satisfaction or disappointment, tipping can often seem like a mysterious ritual with no written rules.

Now more than ever our lives seem busier and as a result we want faster and better service. As we demand more services, there are, in turn, more people to tip. Suddenly a short list of tipping recipients that was once limited to hairdressers, cabbies, waiters, and hotel doormen has expanded to include everyone from dog groomers to the cashiers at your local coffeehouse. Deciding whether to tip for these basic services has become a bewildering process.

We all want to be courteous and do the right thing when it comes to thanking someone for good service, but you have the right to know what you are paying for, what the appropriate tip is, and how not to waste your hard-earned cash. The *Itty Bitty Guide to Tipping* pulls the curtain back on the mystery of tipping, clarifies how to tip for any service, and informs you regarding when it's not necessary to tip at all. Never again do you have to be in that uncomfortable situation of wondering when, whom, and how much to tip. This guide also offers examples of a few scenarios when undertipping is justified. Whether you are paying your waiter or baby-sitter, never again do you have to be an unprepared or uninformed tipper.

Here are tips and advice direct from working people in the service industry. Fun trivia, witty quotes, and job profiles give you a better understanding of exactly what service that person in the uniform actually performs.

How you express your appreciation (or lack thereof) will be remembered by the people who provide you with their services. The greater your show of appreciation, the greater the likelihood that you'll receive excellent service from them in the future. The *Itty Bitty Guide to Tipping* gives you that critical edge to help you become an effective, skillful, and self-assured tipper.

"A fair tip, or one on the generous side, will leave a pleasant feeling and respect for you in the one who receives it. A lavish one will create a secret disrespect and add to the reputation Americans have for trying to buy their way into everything." —*Eleanor Roosevelt*

ITTY BITTY
history of
tipping

The origin of the practice of tipping is unclear, but it may have begun in the late Middle Ages with the idea that a sum of money might be given in exchange for something extra, whether it be services or effort. Some books state that in sixteenth-century England, bar "tavern" patrons would toss coins off the table to get better service. Another story claims that European feudal lords threw money to peasants in the streets to ensure safe passage for themselves. Other theories hold that the word *tip* comes from the Dutch word *tippen*, which may originate from the sound of a coin being tapped against a glass to get a waiter's attention. A few theories hold that the word derives from the Latin word *stips*, meaning "gift." It is also said that the word *tip* made its way into the English language around 1756 in a London pub, where a table held a bowl marked with the words *To Insure Promptitude*. From the first letter of each word, the phrase was abbreviated to *tip*.

In many languages, the word for tip is associated with drinking, since in many cultures the practice of tipping began as an offer to enable the tippee to buy himself a drink. In French the word *pourboire* means "for drink"; the German word *trinkgeld* translates literally to "drink money." We may reasonably guess that the word *tip* is a short form of *tipple*, meaning "to drink."

dining out

Whether you're dining in style at a five-star restaurant or grabbing a burger and beer at your local bar, tipping will be part of your dining experience. For the restaurant staff, your tip is a direct and vital report card for their overall level of service. But how much should you tip, when, and to whom? Read on for a list of the people you will encounter and profiles of the services they provide, together with the lowdown on exactly how much to tip. The tipping chart on pages 24 to 25 provides a quick reference.

the players

When dining out, you have a team working directly to serve you. The fancier the restaurant, the more people there are who will expect a tip. The primary tip (often the only tip) goes to the server, who in turn, at the end of each shift, tips out the bus person, the bartender, and in some places the host. The server is required to pay taxes on the tips that are left over after he or she has tipped out.

The restaurant's tipping-out policies aside, some establishments require servers to declare 15 percent of their total gross sales whether they are tipped 15 percent or not. Restaurants often adhere to this practice to protect themselves in the event of an audit. When restaurants employ a large number of people, servers must often tip out more than 25 percent of their gross tips to the members of their "team." The following is a list of everyone on the team, the services you can expect from them, and a few guidelines to observe.

SERVER : 15%-20%

The server's basic duties include answering questions about the menu; taking your order; delivering your food and drink promptly; and bringing necessities such as condiments, napkins, and an extra plate to the table in a courteous manner. Your server should check back to see if everything is all right or if you need anything else and should present the bill in a timely fashion at the end of your meal. The server should never disappear for long; he or she should stay nearby in case you need another drink or the check.

If these services are performed well, a tip of at least 15 percent is justified. Always tip your server at the end of the meal when you are paying the bill. Tip on the total amount before tax. When paying cash, take the tip from the change you receive and

"Sure it's great when someone tips big, but I'd prefer they left 15 percent and said, 'Thank you,' and 'Have a nice day,' than to leave a large tip and act like I'm not human. Appreciation can be conveyed in more ways than just money." —Joao, server

leave it on the table. If you feel you have received exceptional service, it's nice to hand the tip to your server directly and say thank you. When paying by credit card, fill in the tip amount on the credit slip and leave it on the table. If you have a server who provides you with especially attentive or helpful service such as assisting with elderly guests, accommodating special food requests, or helping you get your children seated and settled in, tip him or her extra.

Certain situations call for extra tipping. A server or host who anticipates your needs or spends extra time assisting someone at your table, perhaps helping your elderly aunt with her coat, or bringing your kids crayons or toys, deserves added recognition from you. And remember, an extra tip doesn't always have to be paid in cash. Notes, cards, and letters to the management are appreciated.

good behavior

A LITTLE EXTRA FOR

BARTENDER : 15%-20%, OR $1 PER DRINK

The bartender's job is to mix and serve drinks at the bar in a courteous and timely manner. If he or she does this, tip him or her when you receive each drink. When you tip a bartender generously on the first round, he or she will keep an eye on your drink, remember what you are drinking, and serve you right away when you order your next round. When you don't tip after the first round, expect slower service on every round thereafter. Now, if you don't like your drink, wait until the bartender is free, explain what the problem is, and ask if he or she would kindly remix it. If the bartender listens and fixes

THE ART OF **complaining**

When bringing a problem to the attention of the manager, try to avoid making grandiose demands or causing a scene. You'll be much more effective if you state your complaint in a direct yet friendly manner. Be specific about what went wrong. Most managers will be receptive if they are approached in this way.

the problem graciously, tip upon receiving the remixed drink. If the bartender ignores you, or if it takes forever to remix your drink, don't tip. When you sit at the bar while waiting for a table, tip after each round. If you opt to run a tab and have it transferred to your dinner bill, give the bartender your final tip when you leave the bar. In many restaurants, bartenders get the short end of the stick—often people forget to tip the bartender at all.

BUS PERSON : NO TIP

A server's right-hand man, the bus person brings you a basket of bread, refills your water glass, removes dirty plates, and brings you extra items. Any server will tell you that the performance of a bus person can make or break the money pot for the night. As a customer, you aren't obligated to tip a bus person directly, but if he or she has been especially attentive (for example, helps get a child into a high chair or brings your drink from the bar without being asked), then you can give a few dollars directly to him or her at the end of your meal, or you can let the management know that you received good service from that person.

SOMMELIER : 20%

A sommelier can put a sparkle into a fine dining experience. With extensive knowledge of the wine list, the sommelier can suggest the perfect wine to pair with your meal. A good sommelier will offer an excellent wine suggestion that is within price range, and check in with you to see if you need anything else. You can tip him or her personally at the end of your meal or let your server know that you are leaving a specific amount for the sommelier. Base your tip on the cost of wine before tax.

COUNTER PERSON : 15%-20%

A counter person's job is identical to that of a server. You can expect the same service sitting at the counter as you would while sitting at a table in the restaurant. Always tip the counter person at the end of the meal the same you would tip at a table. Tip on the total amount excluding taxes. If you are simply picking up a take-out order, tip 10%.

COAT-CHECK & WASHROOM ATTENDANTS : NO TIP

Coat-check attendants store your coat, umbrella, or any bulky items you don't want to keep with you at your table. Washroom attendants keep the restrooms tidy and the toiletries replenished. The fee for checking a garment or other item is often around $1 per item. You are not expected to tip beyond the cost of checking the coat, nor are you required to tip the washroom attendant. If a coat-check attendant stores a large number of shopping bags or a wet umbrella for you, then tip him or her. If a washroom attendant helps you sew on a button or remove a stain, tip him or her a dollar upon completion of the service.

Servers who kneel down next to the table while talking with customers, and make eye contact, improve their tips by 3 percent, from 15 percent to 18 percent. Women servers who write "Thank you" or draw a happy face on the back of their checks receive tips of about 18 percent, whereas male servers who draw a happy face on their checks decrease their tips by 3 percent.

itty bitty trivia

HOST/MAÎTRE D' : NO TIP

The title maître d' is short for *maître d'hôtel* (master of the house), and this person oversees the functioning of the house (the dining area of the restaurant), organizes reservations, assigns tables, and seats guests. While you are not expected to tip the maître d', if you want to be seated without a reservation, or get a great table on a busy night, tip at the beginning of the evening. If you request help coordinating a special occasion such as a marriage proposal, tip him or her $5 to $10 at the end of the evening. You can also acknowledge exceptional service with a thank-you note. This is a wise move if you're a regular—it can put you on the restaurant's A-list.

PARKING VALET : $2

The parking valet is responsible for assisting you in and out of your car, parking your car safely, and, when you are ready to leave, bringing your car in a timely manner. Tip your valet when he or she brings your car. For special requests such as keeping the car parked in front, tip as you make the request. If it's raining or snowing, or if the valet accommodates a special request, then tip up to $5.

Every now and then you'll run across a server better suited for a less people-oriented job, say, graveyard security, who somehow made his way to your table instead. If your server is blatantly rude or disappears on a long cigarette break during your meal, he does not deserve a tip. If your food arrives at your table cold, you receive the wrong order, or your server is entirely unavailable to you, then you did not receive good service. However, before stiffing an impolite or negligent waiter, consider speaking with the management first. Remember, stiffing a surly waiter means that the rest of the team gets stiffed, too! Give the manager the chance to make it up to you. If the manager fixes the problem, comps all or part of your meal (gives it to you free of charge), or genuinely apologizes, tip 15 percent. If the manager dismisses you or makes excuses for the server's bad performance, then you can dismiss the restaurant. Let them know you will not be returning and do not leave a tip.

An honest mistake does not count as a no-tip situation, especially if you are compensated in some way. For example, if a server spills wine on you, that's an honest (though annoying) mistake. If he apologizes, comps some or all of your meal, and offers to pay for cleaning your shirt, that service warrants a tip.

is there such a thing as a no-tip situation?

SERVER
15%–20% OF BILL BEFORE TAX

Assisting with large groups or being helpful with children or elderly guests is considered exceptional service. You can also thank your server personally or let the management know how happy you are with that person's service.

BARTENDER
15%–20% OF BAR BILL BEFORE TAX, OR $1 PER DRINK

Tip $2 to $3 if your bartender is especially entertaining or cheerfully remixes a drink that doesn't taste right.

BUS PERSON
NO TIP

Tip $2 to $3 if your bus person goes above and beyond the call of duty.

SOMMELIER
20% OF WINE BILL BEFORE TAX

Tip 10% more for a superb or budget-wise recommendation.

COUNTER PERSON
15%–20% OF BILL BEFORE TAX
10% FOR TAKE-OUT ORDERS

If the person at the counter provides speedy service, tip $1 to $2 extra.

COAT-CHECK ATTENDANT
NO TIP; $1 PER ITEM IF COAT CHECK IS FREE

If there is a charge for coat check, no tip is necessary —unless you check more than one item. Tip $1 per additional item.

WASHROOM ATTENDANT
NO TIP

Tip $1 to $3 for service above and beyond the call of duty.

HOST, MAÎTRE D'
NO TIP

Tip $5 to $10 for taking care of an unusual request, seating you without a reservation on a busy night, or giving you VIP treatment.

PARKING VALET
$2 PER CAR

Tip at least $5 for accommodating special requests such as front-row parking.

transportation

Getting from here to there, whether for pleasure or business, is a necessary and unavoidable part of modern life. Many people are involved in getting you from point A to point B. This chapter explains how to tip those who help you reach your destination, be it across town or across the continent. How you tip will depend on the type of transportation you choose and the quality of service you receive along the way. Included in this chapter is information on tipping drivers of all sorts, as well as the staff you'll encounter during air and train travel. Read on for specific profiles of people in the transportation industry and refer to the Transportation Tipping Chart on pages 34 to 35 for a short breakdown of tipping practices.

the players

From the skycap who helps you check your large bags to the taxi driver who makes sure you arrive on time, they all help to make your journey safe, timely, and hassle-free. Tip them for their service, as you would a waiter or bartender, and keep in mind, the more expensive the mode of transportation the more you will be expected to tip.

CABDRIVER : 10%

In an ideal situation, you give a cabdriver an address and he or she gets you there without a hitch. This is rudimentary service. Now, if you get a driver who actually has a (good) personality, assists with luggage, or agrees to makes an extra stop on the way for a bottle of wine, that's good service.

But what if you get an awful cabbie? If you end up with a bitter, resentful driver who gets lost or, worse, scares you, then don't feel obliged to tip at all. Instead, contact the cab company and file a complaint.

"When I find a cabdriver I like, I ask if he has a cell phone or number he can be reached at for service. This way I call him directly—he lets me know when he can pick me up and is almost like my own private driver. This has saved me so much time, and I never have to be stuck on hold again!"
—Anastasia, TV producer

AIRPORT SKYCAP : $2 PER BAG

Who can save the day when you're running a little late for a flight? Skycaps can. Their job is to make sure your luggage gets from the curb to the terminal. And at airports where this service is still permitted, they will check your bags, confirm your reservation, and get your luggage on its way to the correct plane. A speedy check-in can mean the difference between catching and missing your flight.

If you need quick service from a skycap, have cash in hand and signal him discreetly by raising your hand, indicating that you are in a hurry and would love some assistance, pronto! The key to getting served right away is to be friendly and direct, not rude. If you get served immediately and efficiently, consider this good service. Tip your skycap after your bags are placed on the cart or belt, or after they have been checked.

AIRPORT CART DRIVER / WHEELCHAIR ASSISTANT : $2–$3 PER PERSON

Airport cart drivers assist persons who, for any of a variety of reasons, need to be transported by cart while at the airport. These drivers, as well as wheelchair assistants, should be quick to assist you and get you to your destination in a timely manner. If they are especially courteous, help with your luggage, and perhaps even stop to get you a soda on the way to the gate, this is great service. Tip upon arriving at your destination, in cash.

TOUR GUIDE : $1–$10 PER DAY

A tour guide may be with you for a single excursion or an entire vacation. Guides should have extensive knowledge about the place you're visiting and answer your questions about the site. Each guide should be tipped at the end of the tour. If a gratuity is already included in the total price of the tour, you do not have to tip unless you feel the service was outstanding. When a guide remembers your name or interests, makes a great site-seeing suggestion, or takes care of any special needs you may have, this is exceptional service. Tip your guide at the end of the day, in cash.

SHUTTLE-BUS DRIVER : 15%

Shuttle drivers take you from one location to another. If it's a free shuttle, no tip is necessary; it is nice, however, to verbally thank a driver, especially one who helps with your bags. If you're paying for shuttle service, the driver should pick you up and drop you off on time and answer any questions you may have about your drive. Tip when you exit the bus. You can tip in cash or include your tip on the credit card slip. A driver who carries your luggage to or from your door or assists with bulky items provides first-rate service and should get an extra $1 to $2 per bag.

Shortly after the introduction of rented luggage carts bearing the name Smarte Cartes at John F. Kennedy International Airport, the number of porters decreased from eighty-nine to sixty-four. When one traveler, pulling a rented cart, reportedly asked one of the remaining porters for directions, the porter is said to have replied, "Your cart says it's smart. Why not ask it?"

ITTY GITTY
trivia

LIMOUSINE OR CAR-SERVICE DRIVER : 15%–20%

A limousine or car service should provide a polite driver who arrives promptly, opens and shuts your door, assists with bags, and describes the car's amenities. Most limousine companies and car services include gratuity in the fare. You can elect to tip more if the driver is particularly courteous, turns a blind eye to your unseemly antics in the backseat, or makes several stops for you during an all-night romp. If you spontaneously share a ride with strangers, don't pool your tips; instead, tip separately. Give the driver his or her tip in cash when you exit the car.

ITTY BITTY trivia

In the 1890s, the New York Central Railroad took pains to inform its customers that porters paid by the company should not be tipped. In order to distinguish employees from "freelancers" hoping for a tip from passengers, the company outfitted them with a special uniform, a distinctive feature of which was a red cap.

TRAIN REDCAP OR PORTER : $1-$2 PER BAG, OR SERVICE

The redcap, or baggage porter, helps you board, lifts your luggage onto the train, and gets you settled in your berth or seat. A sleeping porter is assigned to your area on overnight journeys. When a porter brings you a newspaper, gives you a wake-up call, or is just generally friendly and attentive, this is considered excellent customer service and you can tip up to $5. Do so at the time of service.

TRAIN DINING-CAR WAIT STAFF : 15%

Gratuities may be included in the price of meals. If they are not, then tip as you would in a restaurant.

Although it may seem as though you have to hand out quite a bit of cash while in transit, not everyone expects a tip. It is not necessary for you to tip ticket agents, security personnel, flight attendants, or gate agents. If any of these people go out of their way to help you, thank them by writing a letter to their supervisor.

not to tip WHOM

CABDRIVER
10% OF TOTAL FARE

If your driver helps with baggage, makes an extra stop at your request, or offers a helpful suggestion when asked, tip 15% to 20%.

AIRPORT SKYCAP
$2 PER BAG; $2–$3 MORE FOR HEAVY LUGGAGE

For immediate service, tip $5 to $20 depending on number and size of bags.

AIRPORT CART DRIVER / WHEELCHAIR ASSISTANT
$2–$3 PER PERSON

If the assistant makes extra stops at your request, or waits with you until your party arrives or until you board your plane, give $1 to $2 more.

TOUR GUIDE
$1–$10 PER DAY (IF GRATUITY IS NOT INCLUDED)

For private tours, tip $5 to $10 per outing. For an unusual excursion, for example, parasailing on a private boat, tip 20% of the excursion fee.

SHUTTLE-BUS DRIVER
15% OF TOTAL FARE

*Also, tip $1 to $2 per bag if the driver helps you with
your luggage.*

:::

LIMOUSINE OR
CAR-SERVICE DRIVER
15%–20% (IF GRATUITY IS NOT INCLUDED)

*Tip $10 to $20 more for special requests. If you share
the car service with others, tip 15% of the total fare
per person.*

:::

TRAIN REDCAP OR PORTER
$1–$2 PER BAG OR SERVICE

*For oversize or heavy luggage, or outstanding customer
service, tip $5 or more.*

:::

TRAIN DINING-CAR WAIT STAFF
15% (IF GRATUITY IS NOT INCLUDED)

*For exceptional service, such as arranging a birthday
surprise, tip $3 to $4 more.*

003

Lodging

Employees of all hotels, whether big or small, deluxe or budget friendly, want you to enjoy your stay so you might return or tell a friend about the place. Any experienced traveler knows that the quality of one's stay is in the hands of the hotel staff. Unfortunately, most people forget to budget for tips as they plan their trip. To avoid surprises, include tipping in your budget ahead of time, and tuck fifteen to twenty $1 bills into your pocket to cover your tips upon arrival. Read on for profiles of the staff members you may encounter during your stay, along with advice on when and how to tip them appropriately. Turn to pages 44 to 45 for a quick-reference tipping chart.

the players

When staying at a hotel there is a whole range of services and people available to you—from the doorman who welcomes you and assists you with packages to the concierge who gets you in at the most popular restaurant. How you utilize each person and the services they offer varies greatly, as well as the tipping protocol.

While the practice of tipping varies on the type of hotel, familiarizing yourself with who completes each specific service can make your encounters easier and less intimidating. Know who to tip, why you are tipping them, and precisely how much. The more expensive the hotel, the more people there are to tip. Showing your appreciation for staff members' good service will only improve the quality of your stay. If you cannot afford to tip each staff member who offers you service, tip those you encountered the most during your trip or those who were most helpful to you.

DOORMAN : $1–$3

Whether you pull up in a Pinto or a Benz, the doorman is the first person you will encounter at most hotels. He is responsible for opening the car door for you, unloading your luggage, and tagging your bags for delivery to your room. He is also the person who will bring your car to you when you need it or hail a cab for you. If the doorman provides additional services such as delivering shopping bags to your room, calling you when a visitor arrives, or procuring the hotel's house car for you, consider this fine service. If a doorman is inattentive, don't tip him.

THE HIGH-MAINTENANCE guest

Are you a person of multiple needs? If so, introduce yourself to the concierge when you arrive, tipping her a lump sum and letting her know that you may need her services during your stay. A simple gift, a thank-you note, or a letter to her manager afterward will also be greatly appreciated.

$20 is a good tip. A thoughtful gift, however, often bears more value than any dollar amount.

Always tip the doorman upon completion of service. If you don't have the exact amount available, ask him to make change for you on the spot (a much better solution than telling him you'll take care of him later). If you prefer not to have to dole out $1 bills at every turn, you can opt to tip a lump sum upon arrival or departure—just let him know that's what you'll be doing. Keep in mind that you'll probably encounter more than one doorman during your stay. Should you choose to tip upon checking out, tip the doorman who was most helpful to you during your stay. In the event that he is not working that day, place his cash in a sealed envelope and request that the desk clerk deliver it to him.

The Waldorf-Astoria in New York City was the first hotel in the United States to offer room service to guests.

ITTY GITTY
trivia

BELL STAFF : $1–$2 PER BAG

Hotel bell staff have the power to make your hotel
stay a little more special and a lot less of a headache.
These are the folks who schlep your overstuffed baggage up to your room, give you a quick tour of the
accommodations and offer useful tips such as
restaurant and entertainment recommendations and
special features of the hotel's neighborhood. Carry
your own luggage if you so choose (in which case
you do not have to tip the bellman), but don't ask
to borrow the hotel's luggage cart. It's tantamount
to asking a cabdriver to borrow his car. For extra
services or deliveries to your room such as a fax,
toothbrush, newspaper, or off-property amenity (e.g.,
cold medicine), tip $2 to $5 at the time of delivery.

CONCIERGE : $5

Concierges can take care of everything from getting you a lunch reservation at the hottest restaurant to making flight arrangements to obtaining last-minute concert tickets. Tip upon receiving helpful service. A concierge who goes the extra mile for you and gets you hard-to-find theater tickets or puts you on the guest list at an exclusive club should receive a larger tip. Providing directions to the closest bookstore or general hotel information does not warrant a tip.

FRONT-DESK CLERK : NO TIP

The front-desk clerk assists you when you check in to the hotel, makes sure your room reservation is correct, takes your credit card and gives you your room key, and tells you about the hotel's special amenities, such as a buffet breakfast or in-room movies. If he or she upgrades you or coordinates special requests, such as a roll-away bed or crib delivery to your room, you can show your appreciation with a complimentary note to the supervisor.

HOUSEKEEPER : $2–$4 PER NIGHT

Don't forget the people who clean up after you. The housekeeping staff members make your bed, bring in clean towels, replace your toiletries, and empty your trash cans. Services and tips vary depending on the kind of hotel. If you request niceties like extra shampoo, additional towels, or special pillows, tip upon delivery. When you check out, leave a tip for the entire stay on the bedside table or on the pillow. If you recognize your cleaning person as you're walking down the hall, you can always hand over your tip directly and thank him or her in person.

ROOM-SERVICE STAFF : 15%

Room-service waiters bring your food and drink order to your room. Most hotels automatically include the gratuity on the bill; ask what their policy is when you place your order. This gratuity is sometimes divided between the kitchen staff and wait staff. Extra service that calls for a larger tip might include accommodating a request that requires a second trip to your room or setting up a surprise romantic dinner. If the gratuity is not included on the bill, tip the server in cash as he or she leaves the room or write it in on the bill.

POOLSIDE ATTENDANT : $2–$5

Poolside employees can provide you with towels, set up your lounge chair, and take your food or drink order. It's not necessary to tip when someone hands you a towel. But if you know you'll be lounging by the pool for a few days, you can tip the pool attendant a lump sum upon arrival—you'll be sure to get faster service and the chair with the best view. No tip is necessary if you don't order food or drinks or require service from an attendant.

If tipping in person makes you feel uncomfortable, you can always place tips in a sealed envelope with the person's name on it and ask a clerk at the front desk to forward it to the appropriate person. Just make sure to include your name and room number, so the recipient knows who sent the tip.

IT'S OK TO BE

shy

DOORMAN
$1–$3 PER SERVICE

Tip $2 to $3 for hailing a cab or delivering bags to your room.

BELL STAFF
$1–$2 PER BAG

Tip $2 to $5 for a delivery of items such as shopping bags or boxes to your room.

CONCIERGE
$3–$5 FOR MAKING RESTAURANT RESERVATIONS

Tip $10 for making sought-after dinner reservations at a hot restaurant, $20 for booking tours, and $25 or more for hard-to-get items like tickets to a sold-out show.

FRONT-DESK CLERK
NO TIP

If a clerk offers special services or upgrade, send a thank-you note or $5 cash.

HOUSEKEEPER

$2 PER NIGHT; $3–$4 PER NIGHT AT HIGHER-END HOTELS

> *Tip $1 per extra item, such as a rollaway bed or extra pillow.*

ROOM-SERVICE STAFF

15% (IF GRATUITY IS NOT INCLUDED)

> *Add $5 for an elaborate dinner setup.*

POOLSIDE ATTENDANT

$2–$5 FOR BRINGING EXTRA TOWELS OR ATTENDING TO A LARGE GROUP

> *Tip $2 extra for special requests, such as bringing suntan oil or a newspaper.*

personal care

Ah, the price of beauty. From hair coloring to manicures to bikini waxes, a beauty regime may seem relentless at times, but the payoff, of course, is always worth the trouble. When you do walk out of that spa or salon glowing like a Harry Winston pavé diamond ring, reward your transformers in their order of importance to you. Your tip tells that person that you were especially pleased with the service you received. If you can't afford to tip everyone, that's OK—tip the person who spent the most time on you. Read on for a profile of each service provider and guidelines for tipping these individuals, and refer to the Personal Care Tipping Chart on pages 56 to 57 for extra tipping details.

the players

There are several service providers to tip in the beauty world. Always tip the person who spends the most time making you look fabulous. It *is* customary today to tip the owner of a spa or salon when they provide you a service. But remember to tip employees before the owner if you must make that choice.

As many as five people may touch your hair or body in a single visit to a salon, and while it's nice to tip everyone, it isn't always possible or even necessary. Here's the deal: tips are private. Your tip is between you and your beauty service provider only. Once you find a regular stylist, manicurist, or esthetician, tipping them will become routine.

Looking fabulous isn't limited only to the spa or the salon. Your clothes need to be dry cleaned professionally, you occasionally may need a great tailor, and if you have a car, well, it needs to be in top shape, too. Tipping the folks who maintain your wardrobe may not be customary, but thanking them in itty bitty ways will be much appreciated and remembered. And tipping your car-wash attendant is a really good idea, if your car means anything to you at all.

STYLIST, BARBER, OR COLORIST : 15%

Having a bad hair day is grim. But getting I-feel-fabulous hair is reason for a tipping celebration! A stylist who suggests a great do, updates an out-of-style look, or maintains your healthy locks is doing his or her job well. If that person also dishes out great gossip, lends you a sympathetic ear, or stays late to help with a last-minute hair crisis, that's going above the call of beauty duty, and deserves a little extra compensation. Some stylists might even take on the additional role of one-hour therapist while you sit in the chair, so if you've gotten a great cut and great advice, consider it a two-for-one service and tip more. Most salon personnel prefer cash, since credit card tips have to be declared to the IRS as income. Tip when you pay your bill.

ITTY BITTY INSIDER'S
advice

"Bigger tippers don't get better haircuts, but they do get squeezed in on a busy Saturday afternoon."
—Denise, salon manager

STYLIST'S ASSISTANT : $2-$5

These helpful people are usually stylists in training. They are paid as apprentices and therefore rely on cash tips to augment their paltry take-home pay. They assist your stylist or colorist in a variety of ways: shampooing, blow drying, prepping color mixes, serving you tea, sweeping the floor, and so on. Tip the assistant at the time you pay your bill. Salons usually provide small envelopes for tips; ask the receptionist to pass the envelope on to the assistant. Always tip the supporting staff before the owner. Your appreciation for their service will definitely be remembered next time you're in the chair getting coiffed, fluffed, or straightened.

salon owners

TIPPING

Once upon a time, it was considered unnecessary, even rude, to tip the owner of a beauty salon. Today, although never expected, it is becoming the norm. If the owner is the person who provides the service for you and you are satisfied with his or her work, tip that person as you would a regular employee.

MANICURIST OR PEDICURIST : 15%

Manicure and pedicure services differ from one salon to another, and tipping practices vary depending on the type of salon you visit and the level of service you receive. Basic service is as follows: A manicurist should be on time for your appointment, listen to your requests, be knowledgeable about your options, and paint your nails neatly. The tools used should be sanitized and the environment should be clean and comfortable. Many salons prefer you to tip before they apply polish, so that if you need to reach in your purse or wallet, your polish doesn't get messy. You can do so or keep a few dollars out so you can tip after the service. Higher-end salons will allow you to add a tip on your credit card, whereas many smaller places accept only cash. If one person works on your hands and another on your feet, split the tip equally between them.

A pedicurist who repaints your toes because you put your shoes on too soon or rushes out to feed your parking meter should be tipped more for this extra work. And remember, extra tipping is not always about cold, hard cash. Sometimes a nice gesture is enough; saying a simple thank you, writing a kind note, or delivering a favorite beverage at your next appointment can do the trick.

FACIALIST OR ESTHETICIAN : 15%

Sometimes it hurts to be beautiful. Hair removal and facials can certainly be the most painful part of the beauty process. A facialist cleans your pores, exfoliates dead skin cells, and whips your skin into flawless shape. If your facialist administers treatment in a timely and friendly manner in a soothing and clean environment, then tip him or her. If he or she gives you a lengthy neck massage, makes superb skin-care recommendations, or squeezes you in at the end of the day, tip a bit more.

An esthetician's job is to remove unsightly body hair quickly so it hurts as little as possible. He or she is to provide this service on time in an efficient, sanitary, and friendly manner. Tip a little extra if your esthetician shapes your brows to perfection or removes three months' worth of growth, to show your appreciation for the additional time and attention to detail. For all treatments tip at the end of the service.

MASSAGE THERAPIST : 15%

A massage therapist works out the painful knots in your muscles and de-stresses and detoxes your body. Either this person will come to your home to knead your aching muscles or you'll go to his or her place of business. A massage therapist should ask if you have any injuries or pain, administer a massage in a clean and safe atmosphere, and listen to your needs during the massage. This basic massage service calls for a basic tip. A therapist who makes an exception by coming to your house, squeezes you in on a busy day, or agrees to an appointment on his or her day off provides greater service and deserves greater tipping.

If you leave that ultra-trendy salon feeling unsatisfied or, worse, un-pretty, don't tip. If the manicurist or other provider arrives late and does not apologize or is sloppy, inattentive, downright rude, or makes you feel uncomfortable in some way, then don't tip. But don't be afraid to speak up! Let the manager know that you are unhappy with the service and why. They can't improve if they don't know there's a problem.

not to tip WHEN

CAR-WASH ATTENDANT : $2

Car-wash personnel should do a thorough job, no matter what wash option you've chosen. They should complete their work in a reasonable amount of time, leave your seats and radio as they are, and keep your valuables safe (although most car-wash businesses won't take responsibility for lost or damaged goods, a policy we think is bad service). If you roll up in a monstrous SUV, or come with a car covered with mud, then consider tipping more for the extra time it will take to get your car clean.

DRY CLEANER / TAILOR : NO TIP

The services of a trusty dry cleaner and tailor are indispensable for the busy professional on-the-go. Laundry? Who has time for that? Sewing? Who knows how to do that? So whether it's getting a stain out of your favorite shirt or taking in your jeans a notch, these service providers make our lives more manageable. Tipping these folks is neither necessary nor expected. However, if a dry cleaner or tailor has offered you extraordinary service, say they delivered your dry cleaning to your office or rushed an alteration on a busy day, then consider writing them a thank-you note or sending them a small bouquet of flowers or bottle of wine. Remember, tips don't always have to be in cash.

STYLIST, BARBER, OR COLORIST
15%

> *If the service provider squeezes you in on a busy day,
> tip 20%. Tip $3 to $4 more if he or she tosses in a
> free product.*

STYLIST'S ASSISTANT
$2–$5

> *If the assistant suggests a great new gel or must-have
> brush, tip $1 to $2 more. If that same person sham-
> poos and blow-dries your hair, tip $5 total.*

MANICURIST OR PEDICURIST
15%

> *For giving an extra foot massage during treatment,
> remembering your favorite color, or squeezing you in on
> a busy day, tip $2 to $3 more.*

FACIALIST OR ESTHETICIAN
15%

> *If the service provider gives you free products or makes
> helpful suggestions, tip $2 to $4 more.*

MASSAGE THERAPIST
15%

> *Tip 20% for a house call (unless the therapist already
> charges extra for it).*

CAR-WASH ATTENDANT
$2 PER CAR

> Tip $2 to $3 more if you have an SUV, $5 for campers
> or buses.

DRY CLEANER
NO TIP

> If they rush your cleaning order or restore that ancient
> prom dress to mint condition, drop off some flowers or
> a bottle of wine.

TAILOR
NO TIP

> If they rush an alteration, you may send them a small
> gift or thank-you note.

SERVICES PAID BY GIFT CERTIFICATES
15%–20% (IF GRATUITY IS NOT INCLUDED)

> Ask what the fee for the service is when you call to
> make your appointment.

house calls

"We deliver" and "we make house calls" are magic words to the I-need-it-now guy or gal who is short on time or transportation. Whether they provide basic food delivery or entertain your kids at a birthday party, those kind souls who bring convenience to your doorstep make your life a little bit easier. Read on to find out how to tip them. For the House Calls Tipping Chart, see pages 66 to 67.

the players

Home deliveries and house calls come in a variety of forms and so will your tips. How much you tip will depend on the item or service being provided, the cost of the item or service, and the amount of time the service provider spent in your home. A delivery person who brings pizza to your doorstep won't stick around for long (small tip), but the guys bringing your new sofa might spend a lot of time in your home before they leave (larger tip). If you have booked in-home entertainers for a soiree, then tip more for the added convenience. For a rush or last-minute service request, tip more to recognize the accommodating service.

DELIVERY PERSON : $2-$10

Delivery people should arrive at your doorstep with the correct product or order within the time promised. They should be polite, verify your order, and provide a receipt. If they do this, tip them upon completion of service. If your delivery person is rude, doesn't bring what you asked for, or delivers an item that is flawed in some significant way (cold food, for example), don't tip.

Exceptional delivery service might include very specific on-time delivery, early arrival, or remembering a regular request (like extra soy sauce). When the person delivering an appliance or large piece of furniture is extra helpful and careful, he or she should be tipped more generously.

MOVERS : $10

If you asked for extra help or they offered to assist you in moving a large dresser or couch from here to there tip them $5-$10 extra.

PERSONAL CARE PROVIDERS : 15%–20%

Tailors, facialists, massage therapists—these service providers help us save time, look better, and feel more relaxed. We cover these folks in detail in chapter 4, but how to tip those who make their living doing house calls? Answer: the standard tip for the service is fine. If he or she makes an exception by coming to your office or home, tip generously for this first-rate personalized service. Do not feel obliged to tip if your provider arrived late, provided less than thorough service, or made you feel uncomfortable in any way.

BABY-SITTERS : NO TIP

Baby-sitters are not tipped—however, if you called to say you would be 20 minutes late getting home, or request they perform duties beyond their regular tasks (i.e. watch an extra child during a sleepover, cook dinner, or do some fun, extensive project with your kids) tip $5–$8 upon paying them. Always tip in cash. Definitely give sitters a bonus come holiday time—get them a gift certificate from their favorite record or video store or double your average sitter fee.

HOUSE-PARTY ENTERTAINER : 15%

Booking a mariachi band for Cinco de Mayo? Engaging the services of a clown for a kids' party? If you're satisfied with the entertainer's service, tip in cash at the end of the soiree. If the band coaxes even your most reluctant guests to get up and salsa, then tip more. If the person arrives late or doesn't deliver the service promised to you, don't tip. Instead, call the company you booked with and let them know you were not satisfied with the service.

PLAN ahead

Don't get caught without a tip for the magician. Children's parties, bar mitzvah celebrations, and sweet-sixteen bashes can easily become huge productions with astronomical price tags. You can avoid unpleasant surprises by planning ahead for tips when organizing the party. Expect to tip all entertainers, such as DJs, pony wranglers, or clowns 15 to 20 percent of their fee.

BARTENDER / CATERER : 15%

The duty of a bartender hired for a special event is to make drinks for your guests and deliver them in a friendly manner. If he consistently does so throughout the evening, tip 15 percent of the total bar bill. If he goes out of his way and plays with the kids, tells a few entertaining stories, or is helpful with other aspects of the event, compensate him with a 20-percent tip for excellent service.

Caterers should arrive at the event location on time and set up prior to guests arriving. If they provide good service, clean up to your liking, and serve guests in a polite, friendly manner, tip the catering company 15 to 20 percent cash at the end of the event.

It is legal for a U.S. postal worker or letter carrier to accept a cash tip of up to $20.

ITTY BITTY trivia

Twinkling lights adorn the homes in your neighborhood, the smell of gingerbread fills the air, and your brain is buzzing with frantic thoughts of all the gifts you still need to buy. 'Tis the season to remember all those who have helped you throughout the year. From nannies to baby-sitters, gardeners to garbage collectors, you'll want to acknowledge these folks come holiday time. Cash is always welcome, of course, but the holidays are the perfect time to show your appreciation with a thoughtful card or gift instead. You might even consider baking a homemade treat. If you do elect to tip in cash, here's how.

HOLIDAY
tipping

Parking garage attendant: One-third of your monthly bill

Nanny: 1 week's salary plus a small gift from your child

Baby-sitter: An average evening's pay, plus a small gift from your child

Housekeeper: 1 to 2 weeks' salary

Garbage collector: $10 to $20

Newspaper carrier: $5 to $10

Mail carrier: Up to $20

Doorman: $25 to $100

Building superintendent: $30 to $100

Elevator operator: $20 to $50

Personal trainer: Price of 1 session

Dog walker: 1 week's salary

Manicurist: $10 to $50

Hairdresser: $25 to $100

FOOD DELIVERY PERSON

$2

For larger orders, tip $5 or 15% of the bill, whichever is more.

:::

FLOWER DELIVERY PERSON

$2

For larger arrangements or plants, tip $3 to $4 more.

:::

FURNITURE DELIVERY PERSON

$10 (PER DELIVERY PERSON)

If they move other furniture or have to climb stairs, tip $5 to $10 more per delivery person.

:::

MOVERS

$10

Tip $5 to $10 more if they provide extra help.

PERSONAL CARE PROVIDER

15%–20%

> *If the provider squeezes you in on a busy or "off" day,
> or if making a house call is an exception to his or her
> policy, tip more than 20%.*

BABY-SITTERS

NO TIP

> *Tip $5 to $8 if they perform duties beyond their
> regular tasks.*

HOUSE-PARTY ENTERTAINER

15%

> *Tip more if service is outstanding or if the entertainer
> performs longer than scheduled free of charge.*

BARTENDER / CATERER

15%

> *Tip 20% if they accommodate special requests, or
> handle unexpected mishaps well.*

weddings and other special events

It's no secret that many weddings or special events today cost a fortune, and the thought of having to shell out even more dough in the form of tips can cause a host to have a total panic attack. The best bet when coordinating a large event is to factor tips for key service providers ahead of time into your grand total. Read on for a description of services that you're likely to need and see pages 78 to 79 for the easy-to-read Weddings and Other Special Events Tipping Chart.

the players

When coordinating a wedding or other event, plan to tip for the following services: deliveries, transportation, photography, wedding officiating, catering, bartending, entertainment, valet parking, and help in planning the whole thing.

At first glance, a wedding or special event may seem like the type of situation where service people shouldn't expect tips. However, tipping has become a common practice at events and many vendors will expect it. Tipping protocol may vary depending on where you're holding the event and the overall budget. If you're hosting your party at a location commonly used for events, ask the on-site coordinator for guidance in this matter. This chapter focuses on those services particular to a wedding or other large event. Visit the other chapters for the lowdown on general services such as valet parking or personal care.

DELIVERY PERSON : $10

From sound equipment and flowers to linens and rentals, the items you need for your party will come via delivery personnel. Delivery people are in charge of loading their trucks with your goods, driving to and finding your location, and unloading on time. Sometimes tips are included in the fee. Check when you place the order. If tips are not included, tip in cash upon completion of the service.

SERVICE PROVIDERS YOU
don't have to tip

The people listed below traditionally don't accept tips, but you can certainly send a thank-you note for exceptional service.

Owners of businesses
Bridal shop employees
Invitation printers
Florists

DRIVER : 15%-20%

A gratuity is often included in the stated price for renting a limousine or other vehicle. Your driver should be friendly and helpful and pick you up and deliver you to your destination on time. Tip extra for exceptional service such as snapping some photos for you or providing tissues when you get weepy.

PHOTOGRAPHER OR VIDEOGRAPHER : NO TIP

Tipping these folks is optional. If you're paying top dollar for their services, you're not expected to tip.

A POCKET FULL OF tip envelopes

Don't wait until the actual event to think about whom, when, and how much to tip! Sit down and make a list of all potential tippees, then count out cash and insert it into labeled envelopes. This way you can have separation anxiety about parting with your cash at home rather than on the day of the event. It's also a good idea to keep a reserve envelope of extra cash handy just in case you run into any unexpected helpful people along the way.

WEDDING OFFICIANT : VARIES

A clergyperson or other officiant counsels you if necessary, understands the kind of ceremony you expect, and follows through with your agreed-upon wishes. If you're getting married in a house of worship you might consider making a donation to that house of worship in lieu of a tip to the officiant. If you're a member of the congregation and are allowed to use the building free of charge, your tip or donation will depend on your personal relationship with the organization. Ask at the office if they follow any standard procedures for accepting tips or donations, since practices differ greatly between religions and organizations. If you are being wed on a beach or at a private home by someone

TIPPING etiquette

Ask about tipping protocol ahead of time. Before you even think about passing out any hard-earned cash (and before you sign any contracts), speak with the location manager or the wedding or event planner about how tips are typically handled. Ask whether service charges or gratuities are included, since you may not have to tip.

not affiliated with any religious organization, you may elect to give the officiant a personal gift. Thank-you cards and heartfelt notes are also nice ways to acknowledge your officiant.

ENTERTAINER : 15%

Your DJ or band should show up on time, play the music that you have agreed upon, and perform for the period of time stated in your contract. For satisfactory service, give a standard tip. If your DJ goes out of his or her way to help set up a sound link with a video component, for example, give him or her a larger amount to recognize the extra effort.

Avoid extra stress on your big day by appointing someone in your group or bridal party to distribute tips. The host or hostess, wedding coordinator, maid of honor, father of the bride, and best man are all ideal candidates for this task.

DELEGATE TIPPING
duty

WEDDING OR
EVENT PLANNER : GIFT

If you've hired a wedding or event planner, you know that you've entrusted the entire outcome of your event to that person. These professionals are responsible for helping to make your vision a reality. They coordinate countless details, such as the entertainment, floral arrangements, photography, and decor. While it isn't imperative to tip your wedding or event planner (often the owner of the company), you should tip his or her assistants. Many event planners will not accept a cash tip but will appreciate a thoughtful gift.

"When we booked our wedding reception location, we found out that the banquet and bar managers were huge Dodgers fans, so on the day of our dress rehearsal we gave each of them opening day tickets—they were delighted. They took very good care of us, and even threw in a case of wine during the reception, free of charge!"
—Nicole and Denny, newlyweds

BANQUET MANAGER OR CATERER : 15%

The banquet manager or caterer's job is to make sure the appetizers or meal are exactly what you want and are served without a hitch. From the hors d'oeuvres to the dessert, your meal's timing and success are in their hands. Usually a gratuity is included in the contract.

If your event is not being held at a hotel, restaurant, or club, chances are that the staff must work out of a minimally equipped kitchen or tent. When deciding on the gratuity amount, consider whether they have had to traipse up and down stairs, endure bad weather, or wait on rude guests, and tip accordingly. Sometimes a caterer will collect a lump sum and distribute it to the servers, but often the caterer requests that the servers be tipped individually. Whether you are paying the standard tip or offering extra compensation for spectacular service, put cash in a labeled envelope(s) and hand it to the caterer or servers at the end of the event.

EVENT BARTENDER : 15%

A good bartender will serve drinks to guests in a pleasant, relaxed manner. (It's a celebration after all, not a busy night at a dance club!) Check with the caterer or manager to find out whether the gratuity is included in your contract. If your bartender's charming personality creates an enjoyable atmosphere for your guests, you can give him or her a little extra cash at the end of the evening even if the tip is already included in the bill.

DELIVERY PERSON
$10 (PER PERSON, IF GRATUITY IS NOT INCLUDED)

If they are ultra-efficient and polite, or if they offer you a discount, tip $2 to $3 more per person.

DRIVER
15%–20% (IF GRATUITY IS NOT INCLUDED)

Tip $3 or $4 more if the driver is especially attentive or makes extra stops at your request.

PHOTOGRAPHER OR VIDEOGRAPHER
NO TIP

For a truly exceptional job, tip $20 to $25 in cash at the end of the evening or send a thank-you note.

WEDDING OFFICIANT
VARIES

Base the amount of your tip or donation on the guidelines set forth by the house of worship. For example, donate 10% of the cost of your wedding, or $50 to $200, if you are not a member of the congregation and you have had limited involvement with the officiant. Give $50 to $200 or a thoughtful gift to an officiant who is not associated with any house of worship.

ENTERTAINER
15%

Tip $20 more if they performed longer than the time set in their contract.

WEDDING OR EVENT PLANNER
SPECIAL GIFT

Tip the planner's assistant $100. If he or she has more than one assistant, tip $50 each.

BANQUET MANAGER OR CATERER
15%

If the person accommodates unexpected guests or provides superior catering, tip $50 to $100 more.

EVENT BARTENDER
15% (IF GRATUITY IS NOT INCLUDED)

If the bartender is especially charming, helpful, or entertaining, tip $20 to $50 more.

casinos and cruise ships

Vacationing at a casino or on a cruise ship can bring up a host of tipping dilemmas. Stays at these facilities are often marketed as "all-inclusive" packages, so it's often hard to figure out when and whom to tip. This chapter is divided into two sections, one for casinos and one for cruise ships, covering the various services you can expect to encounter on your trip and how and what to tip. See page 91 for the Casinos Tipping Chart and pages 92 to 93 for the Cruise Ship Tipping Chart.

at a casino

How much money you'll tip in a casino will depend upon whether you're winning or losing. The more money you win, the more money you will be expected to tip the employees who help you along the way. Every game has a different tipping protocol. Ask the pit boss or dealer for tipping guidelines—they're usually happy to provide assistance. And remember, dealers aren't the only people who expect a tip. Cocktail wait staff, bartenders, slot changers, and valets are other people to tip in and around the casino world. The following is a breakdown of casino tipping customs.

DEALER : $1-$5 PER WIN

The dealer is the person who directly facilitates your good fortune. He or she should deal and shuffle cards, make eye contact with you, keep the game moving along, and pay out appropriately as you win. At the tables, how you tip will depend entirely upon whether you're winning or losing. The rules are simple: losers don't have to tip, but winners do. Tip with chips—dealers are rarely tipped in cash unless a player really wins big. To tip the dealer, pass him or her a $1 to $5 chip each time you win. If you hit the jackpot—and we hope you do—tip your dealer when you cash out. Instead of doling out a tip, you can also play an extra hand on behalf of the dealer next to your bet.

BAR STAFF : $1-$2 PER DRINK

Cocktail servers bring you free drinks and sometimes cigarettes while you play. Tip per drink each time they serve you.

PIT BOSS : NO TIP

A pit boss is the unofficial manager of the casino. He oversees everybody else: the dealers and the players, and especially anyone who looks like trouble. In addition to offering advice about how to play the game, the pit boss acts as a liaison between big players and the house. Tip only for special services such as arranging liberal credit for you, giving you a hotel room or an upgrade, or procuring tickets to a sold-out show.

SLOT ATTENDANT : $1

Slot attendants usually float around the slot machine area. Their job is to make change, oversee the slot machines, and, of course, assist you when you win big. Tip an attendant in cash at the time of the service.

on a cruise ship

This section covers the tipping etiquette on the high seas. Some cruise ships discourage tipping altogether, while others facilitate tipping by providing tiny envelopes specifically for the purpose. Ask your travel agent or cruise-line representative about tipping policies prior to boarding and preferably before buying your tickets. If your cruise ship is the kind that condones tipping, pack a stash of small bills so you don't run out of tip money during your cruise. The money you need to estimate for tips may range from $20 to $200, depending on the length of your cruise, the level you lodge on, and the class of your cruise ship. During your cruise, you'll encounter wait staff, bartenders, stewards, and other service providers who'll help you relax, serve you cocktails and food, and keep you entertained. Here are some basics on tipping these professionals.

PORTER : $1 PER BAG

Porters help load your luggage onto the ship and direct it to your cabin, just as a bellman does in a hotel. Tip per bag at the time of service.

CABIN STEWARD : $3–$5

Your cabin steward is charged with keeping an assigned group of rooms tidy and bringing you any extra items you request. The cruise's level of luxury will determine how much you'll tip.

At the beginning of the cruise, get the names of the ship's staff and write their names on tip envelopes so your tips will go to the right people. You can save time by placing estimated cash tips in these envelopes at the onset of your trip. You can add or take away at the end of your trip once you have evaluated the service you receive.

GET A JUMP ON tipping

BUTLER : $5-$10 PER DAY

If you are booked on the top deck in a suite or your cruise ship offers the utmost in luxury, then you may have a butler. This person is assigned to only a few cabins or suites and makes himself or herself available to meet your needs and take care of any special requests you may have. He or she will unpack your things, ensure that your cabin is always well-appointed and stocked with proper amenities, serve you drinks, and handle personal requests such as delivering faxes to your room or bringing you a specific type of pillow.

DECK STEWARD : $1-$2 PER SERVICE

You'll be spending a lot of time on deck. A deck steward stands by, ready to take your food or drink order, bring you a newspaper or towel, and provide information about activities on board. A steward should be tipped for delivering drinks or a magazine and a little extra if he or she helps you find your lost sun hat or brings you suntan lotion from the gift shop. Tip at the time of service. You don't need to tip for basic services such as providing a towel or giving directions.

EXCURSION PLANNER OR CONCIERGE : $5-$10 PER SERVICE

An excursion planner can help plan activities, book mini-tours, and make reservations for you both while on board and while the ship is docked at ports. If this person consistently offers fantastic recommendations for activities, shops, or sites, then tip after each service he or she provides. Or you may want to set aside the cash for each tip in an envelope at the beginning of the cruise and hand it to him or her as you return from your excursions. A truly great recommendation, such as directions to a restaurant in a tiny Mexican town that served the best chicken mole you've ever tasted, deserves special notice and added compensation. If a planner doesn't provide you with any service, no tip is necessary.

cruise ship Dining

If you elect to eat buffet style across the board, you probably won't be tipping anyone in the dining room. Of course, you'll tip a server who goes to the kitchen to take care of an unusual request (e.g., you're allergic to mayonnaise and want tuna salad made with mustard instead). Most cruises, however, offer more formal dining options, especially at dinner. If you're cruising in deluxe style, you will be assigned to a table and be served by the same maitre d', headwaiter, sommelier or bartender, and other wait staff members every night. If tips aren't included, bring plenty of cash for tips with you. The fancier the cruise, the more people there will be to tip at dinner. If your cruise ship line discourages tipping, then no need to tip.

MAITRE D': $5

In restaurant hierarchy the maitre d' is in charge of the entire dining world. He's responsible for congenially overseeing your section and its team of servers, bus persons, and sommeliers. He makes sure the whole team is working for you with efficiency, speed, and courtesy. Tip him on the last night of your cruise if he has gone out of his way to ensure that you enjoyed your meals or has given you extra attention during your trip—for example, remembering your name and specific likes or dislikes.

Try to tip on Friday nights if you are on a cruise of two weeks or more. This way, the tippee has some extra cash to spend during his or her time off when you dock at ports.

FRIDAY NIGHT IS
tipping night

SERVER : $2–$5 PER DAY

Servers should provide knowledgeable suggestions and deliver your food in a timely and friendly manner, checking in with you periodically and unobtrusively throughout the meal. The servers oversee the bus persons, who in turn work with the kitchen staff, assisting with serving and cleanup. You have a team working to provide you orderly and courteous table service. If the team succeeds, reward them. If one part of the team lags, for example, a bus person continually neglects to refill your water glass, but everyone else offers smashing service, tell your server and allow him or her to fix the situation, but still tip as you would without the problem.

Instead of tipping every night, pay each person separately at the end of your last meal on board. Place cash tips in sealed envelopes marked with the names of the recipients. If you prefer, you may give all the envelopes to the maitre d' to distribute.

CASINO DEALER
$1–$5 PER WIN

Tip 5% to 10% of winnings or play a hand next to yours for the dealer.

:::

BAR STAFF
$1 PER DRINK FOR BARTENDER
$1–$2 PER DRINK FOR COCKTAIL SERVER

Tip $2 to $5 more per drink in swankier locales if you win big.

:::

PIT BOSS
NO TIP

Tip $20 for a free or upgraded room; for free tickets, tip 10% to 15% of ticket value.

:::

SLOT ATTENDANT
$1 FOR CHANGE; $3 FOR FIXING A MACHINE

If you win big, tip 10% of winnings.

PORTER
$1 PER BAG

For extra-heavy luggage, tip $2 to $3 per bag.

CABIN STEWARD
$3–$5 PER DAY (IF YOU HAVE DAILY CONTACT)

Tip $2 to $3 more for special requests, or for carrying shopping bags.

BUTLER
$5–$10 PER DAY

For making special arrangements, tip $20.

DECK STEWARD
$1–$2 PER SERVICE

Tip 15% of bar bill if you get special attention.

EXCURSION PLANNER OR CONCIERGE
$5–$10 PER SERVICE

For consistently exceptional shopping or sight-seeing suggestions, tip $20 at the end of the cruise.

MAITRE D'

$5 PER DAY (IF YOU HAVE PLEASANT CONTACT)

Tip $20 if he helps arrange a private setup for a marriage proposal or birthday surprise.

:::

SERVER

$2–$5 PER DAY

Tip $5 for stellar service, e.g., he or she always remembers your favorite drink or salad dressing.

:::

BUS PERSON

$1–$2 PER DAY PER PERSON

Tip $2 more if he or she helps to clean up a messy spill.

:::

SOMMELIER

$2–$5 PER DAY

Tip 10% of bottle price if suggestion was outstanding.

:::

BARTENDER

$1–$3 PER DRINK

Tip $2 to $3 extra if he or she remembers your drink as you approach the bar or if you make a special request. Tip $5 if he comps your drink.

going abroad

Whether you're hitting the open road on a short trip to Mexico or taking Europe by storm, tipping etiquette abroad varies quite a bit. In this chapter you'll learn about basic tipping customs around the world.

Tipping as a concept is still frowned upon in many countries, but it is becoming more accepted in most big cities. When visiting European countries, read your restaurant bill closely. Oftentimes a 10 to 15 percent gratuity has automatically been tacked onto your total. It is customary, however, to leave a few extra euros for a waiter, bartender, or hotel staff member who has served you particularly well. When traveling in developing countries, prepare to tip well, preferably in American greenbacks. Tipping your driver or guide in American dollars can mean a ride in a better car, an invitation to an out-of-the-way locale, or a photo of a site that typically doesn't permit pictures. Tips may also influence locals to offer up helpful advice on safety and customs, streets to avoid, how to ask for help, and general navigation. Avoid gratuity-related mishaps by reading the advice in the Going Abroad Tipping Chart on pages 96 to 111, which provides a partial list of countries. If you don't see your destination here, a good travel agent can give you some guidelines.

going abroad tipping chart

AUSTRALIA AND NEW ZEALAND

Tipping is not prevalent in restaurants or bars but is becoming more common in large cities. Tip porters US$1 per bag. Give waiters 10% to 15%. Guides and hired drivers don't expect tips, but if you are satisfied with their service tip US$4 to $5. Taxi drivers don't expect to be tipped, but you can leave extra change for good service.

FIJI AND TAHITI

Tipping is not expected in these countries. If you receive exceptional service at a restaurant or hotel, give 10% to the staff member who helped you or ask the management if there is a shared tipping fund you could contribute to.

GUAM

While this island may be small and distant, it is a U.S. territory, so American customs apply here. Tip as you would in the States.

ANTIGUA, ARUBA, BAHAMAS, BERMUDA, AND JAMAICA

Hotels and restaurants usually add a 15% service charge to the bill. If you're pleased with the service you receive leave another 5%. Taxi drivers expect a 10% tip; porters and bell staff expect about US$1 to $2 per bag. Housekeepers are not usually tipped, but if you feel you have received excellent service, tip US$2 to $3 per night.

ARGENTINA

In bars and restaurants, leave 15%, tip bellmen and doormen at least one peso. Taxi drivers don't really expect tips, but if you receive good service, tip a few pesos.

BARBADOS

Drivers of metered taxis expect a 15% tip. Fees for unmetered transport should be negotiated in advance. Porters expect $1 to $2 per bag from foreigners. Most hotels automatically add a 15% service charge to your bill. Additional maid service tips may also be added to your hotel bill at a rate of $1 to $2 per day.

BELIZE

A service charge of 10% is included on the bill at bars and restaurants. Other service workers, hotel staff, and cabbies don't expect any tips.

BRAZIL

Restaurants add a 10% service charge to the check, but it's customary to give one's server an additional 5% tip. If no service charge is added onto the bill, tip 15%. In luxury hotels, tip bell staff US$1 per bag, housekeepers 50 cents a day, and parking valets US$1. If a taxi driver assists you with luggage, he will charge you about 35 cents per bag in addition to the fare; in general, tip them 10% of the fare.

BRITISH VIRGIN ISLANDS

As on the U.S. mainland, tipping of 15% to 20% is customary for service well done. Some hotels automatically add a service charge, there is no need to tip staff above this. Baggage handlers are normally tipped up to US$1 per bag. Most restaurants add a 15% service charge automatically to your bill. You do not have to tip more unless service was outstanding. Taxi drivers are tipped 10%.

CANADA

Tips and service charges are not usually added to the bill in Canada. In general, tip as you would in the States, 15% to 20%, in Canadian dollars.

CAYMAN ISLANDS

At larger hotels, a 7% to 10% service charge is usually included on the bill. In smaller establishments tipping is up to you. Although tipping is customary in restaurants, some businesses automatically include gratuities, so review your tab closely. Taxi drivers expect a 10% to 15% tip.

CHILE

Tip 10% of the bill in restaurants. Taxi drivers don't expect to be tipped because most own their own cabs. If you hire a taxi for a tour, tip the driver 20%. In hotels, tip bell staff and doormen US$1.

COLOMBIA

Throughout Colombia, a 16% service charge is added to hotel bills. You don't have to tip more. In restaurants, cafés, and bars, a 10% service charge is added. If the service charge isn't included on the bill, the standard tip is 10%.

COSTA RICA

Tip hotel bell staff 50 cents per bag. A 10% service charge is usually added to your hotel or restaurant bill. Taxi drivers are not usually tipped.

GUATEMALA

Tipping is expected. In more expensive restaurants and hotels, tip 15% unless a service charge has already been added to the bill. You do not have to tip taxi drivers.

MARTINIQUE

A service charge of 10% (service compris) *is added to most hotel and restaurant bills in larger towns and tourist areas, but it's customary to add another 5% to 10% for exemplary service. If the* service compris *hasn't been added, the standard tip is 10% to 15% at restaurants. Tip hotel bellmen US$1 per bag. Tip taxi drivers 10%.*

MEXICO

Many tourist industry workers in Mexico expect to be tipped in U.S. dollars. Tip bell staff $1 per bag at lower or moderately priced hotels, $2 per bag at more expensive hotels. Tip housekeepers $1 per night at lower priced hotels, $3 to $5 at higher-end resorts. Tip 10% at bars and restaurants, and give $1 or a few pesos to cabdrivers who are helpful.

PERU

In this country restaurants are supposed to print prices, including service charges, on their menus. In fact, some establishments may add a service charge for everything from entertainment to extra dressing for your salad. If service prices are not printed, tip 10%. Ask the host or server what the service charges are before you order or when you sit down. Hotels will add a 10% service charge to your bill. It is not customary to tip more.

PUERTO RICO

Some hotels add a 10% to 15% service charge to the bill. Ask whether the service charge is included in your room rate. Tips are expected and appreciated; tip porters and bell staff US$1 per bag, servers 15% to 20%, maids US$2 to $3 per day, and taxi drivers 10% to 15% in U.S. dollars.

U.S. VIRGIN ISLANDS

Most hotels include a 10% service charge to cover housekeepers and other staff, but some hotels may not actually pass the gratuity on to staff, using it instead to fund their operations. Ask your bell staff, servers, and housekeepers; if you discover that they do not receive gratuities from their employers tip US$1 to $2 per bag to porters, wait staff 15%, and housekeepers US$2 to $3 per day.

CHINA

Once unheard of, tipping has now become more common in China. Tip 4% to 5% of the bill in restaurants. In larger cities like Shanghai or Hong Kong, a 10% service charge is added to the hotel bill. Tip bellhops US$1 per bag, and you can let cab drivers keep leftover change. The CTS tour guides are not permitted to accept tips, but they love American products such as stickers, shirts, and cigarettes.

INDIA

India is a country that runs on tips. Tip bellhops US$1 per bag and housekeeping US$1 to $3 per night depending on how expensive your hotel is. Tip 10% to restaurant and room-service waiters. Give porters at the airport US$1 per bag. Taxi drivers don't expect tips but you can give them some change if they go out of their way to help you.

INDONESIA

In bigger cities like Jakarta, Bali, and Surabaya, high-end hotels charge a 21% tax. Above this hotel service charge, plan to tip bell staff US$1 per bag. Tip US$2 per bag at more expensive hotels. Most bars and restaurants add on a 10% service charge to your bill. If they don't, tip 10%. Tip airport porters US$1 per bag.

Taxi drivers expect the leftover change from your fare. Tip private drivers US$5 for a half day and $10 for a full day. In smaller cities, don't tip at all.

JAPAN

Tipping is generally not accepted in Japan. There is no need to tip hotel employees or waitstaff. In restaurants, a 10% to 15% service charge is already added to the bill. Don't tip above that. In bars and nightclubs tips are not expected, but feel free to contribute to a tip jar, if any. If you hire a driver for one day there is no need to tip, but if you use him for a few days you can tip what seems appropriate. Be prepared to have your tip rejected—Japanese culture is still very formal and your offer may embarrass the recipient.

NEPAL

Outside of luxury hotels and restaurants catering to foreign visitors, tipping is not customary and can embarrass the intended recipient. Tip no more than 10% for services in hotels and restaurants. Taxi drivers are not usually tipped.

PHILIPPINES

Most hotels and restaurants add on a 10% service charge. You can tip US$1 to $2 more if you like. Tip porters 50 cents per bag and give taxi drivers spare change.

SINGAPORE

Tipping is discouraged in Singapore. It is not expected in hotels and is prohibited at airports. Restaurants add a 10% service charge, tipping above that is not permitted. Taxi drivers are not tipped.

TAIWAN

Tipping is officially discouraged and can be considered an insult.

THAILAND

Tipping is not common practice in Thailand, and offering tips can embarrass the intended recipient. Travelers should not tip service providers.

VIETNAM

Tipping at restaurants and hotels is not common in Vietnam, although many upscale places are starting to add a 10% gratuity to bills. If this hasn't been done and the service is good, you might consider leaving 5% to 10%. As you go farther north or into rural areas, most service providers will refuse tips altogether.

CZECH REPUBLIC

If a 10% service charge is not already included in your hotel or restaurant bill, go ahead and tip 10%. Taxi drivers also get 10%. Don't leave money on your table but give it directly to your waiter. You can tip a guide or private driver 10%.

DENMARK

Hotels and restaurants usually add a 15% service charge to all bills. It is customary to offer to buy your bartender or host a drink in the absence of a service charge. Porters at first-class hotels and airports receive US$1 to $2 per bag. It is not necessary to tip taxi drivers, although most riders round up the fare.

FINLAND

Restaurants and hotels usually include a 10% service charge. You can tip taxi drivers, bell staff, and porters using your extra change. When no service charge is imposed, tip at your own discretion or 10%.

FRANCE AND BELGIUM

A service charge is included on restaurant and bar bills. If you receive exceptional service, leaving extra change on the table lets your waiter know that you were satisfied. Look out for signs that say "pourboire interdit," which means "tipping is prohibited."

GERMANY AND AUSTRIA

Most bars, restaurants, and hotels include a 10% to 15% service charge on their bills. Tip bellhops the equivalent of US$1 per bag or room-service staff $2. Tip taxi drivers 5%.

GREAT BRITAIN

Most restaurants and hotels add a 10% service charge; if they don't then you can tip 10%. Believe it or not, pub bartenders don't usually receive tips. Tip taxi drivers 10% of the fare and the equivalent of US$1 per bag to bell staff.

GREECE

Service charges are figured into the price of meals, according to law, but unless the waiter is rude it is customary to leave an additional 8% to 10%. During the Christmas and Greek Easter holiday periods, restaurants add an obligatory 18% holiday bonus for the waiters to your bill. Tip porters the euro equivalent of 50 cents to US$1 per bag. In better hotels, tip bell staff

US$1 to $2 per bag and housekeeping US$1 per day. Tip taxi drivers with spare change.

:::

IRELAND

It's customary in Ireland for restaurants and hotels to add a 12% service charge to your bill. Tip servers but not pub bartenders. Offer taxi drivers 10% of the fare and bell staff the euro equivalent of US$1 per bag.

:::

ITALY

Expect to tip the taxi 15% of the fare. Porters usually receive $1 to $2 per piece of luggage. Service charges are applied directly to the hotel bill. However, you could consider leaving the maid $2 to $3 per day per visit at the end of your stay. All restaurants include a cover charge per person (pane e coperto) and often a 12% service charge as well. For excellent service in restaurants, tip the waiter an additional 5%. If a wine steward is involved, tip 10% of the cost of the wine.

:::

NORWAY

A service charge of between 10% and 15% is included in most hotel bills. You can tip porters the equivalent in kronor of US$1 per bag at airports and US$2 per bag at better hotels. Restaurants usually add a gratuity of 10% to 15%. If a gratuity is not included, tip him or her 15%. No tip is expected in taxis, although 5% to 10% is appreciated.

RUSSIA

*Service is often nonexistent in Russia. Hotels will often
add a 5% to 15% service charge as well as a 20% VAT
tax, so you needn't tip staff above that. You may, however, tip porters US$1 per bag. At restaurants it is now
customary to tip good servers 10% to 15%. Taxi drivers
are tipped 10%.*

SPAIN AND PORTUGAL

*Tipping is less common here than in the U.S. and serv-
ice charges are usually added to your bill. At more
expensive hotels or restaurants, you can tip an additional 10% for exceptional service.*

SWEDEN

*Tip 10% at restaurants. At hotels, tip the equivalent in
kronor of US$1 per bag, and give taxi drivers 15%.*

SWITZERLAND

*Service is usually included at hotels and restaurants.
For first-class service, tip an additional 5% to 10%.*

ISRAEL

Tip 10% on top of all service charges. Tip guides and private drivers the equivalent in New Israeli Shekels of US$5 per day.

:::

LEBANON

Tipping is not customary or expected, even if you receive outstanding service.

:::

SAUDI ARABIA

Tips are widely expected here so carry lots of loose change if you want good service. You don't have to tip large sums; it's the gesture that counts. Service is not usually included at restaurants, so tip 10% of the bill.

CENTRAL AFRICA REPUBLIC

Foreign travelers are often perceived as being rich, and tips are expected. At upscale hotels, tip as you would at any luxury hotel in the States, but it is not necessary to tip at more modest establishments. It is fairly standard to tip in the range of 10% at restaurants. Porters can be tipped with change. Taxi drivers do not expect tips, but private drivers are tipped 10% of the fare per day.

EGYPT

You'll be expected to tip everyone, including hotel staff, taxi drivers, porters, guides, servers, and bartenders. Small tips are fine, usually 5% of the bill or US$1 per task performed.

KENYA

Unless a service charge is already added, it is customary to include a 10% tip to hotel bills. Most restaurants include a service charge of 10% on the bills and it is not necessary to tip more. Taxi drivers generally receive a 10% tip. At five-star lodges, tip the tracker, ranger, and innkeeper US$10 per day at the end of a stay.

MOROCCO

Tipping isn't universal here, but in higher-end restaurants or hotels you can tip 10%. The equivalent in Dirham of US$1 per bag for a porter, US$1 a day for the house-keeper, and spare change for a taxi driver are customary tips.

SOUTH AFRICA

No tipping is necessary at hotels that add a 10% service charge. If a service charge is not added, tip 10% to 15%. Many restaurants already add a service charge and do not expect additional tips. If a service charge is not added, you can tip your server 10% to 15%. Taxi drivers customarily get a 10% tip. Porters are tipped the equivalent of 50 cents in rand per piece of luggage. At the end of your stay at a private game lodge, you're expected to tip both the ranger and the tracker. Tipping guidelines vary from lodge to lodge, but plan to give the rand equivalent of about US$10 per person per day to the ranger as well as to the tracker. For a couple stay-ing two days, tip US$25 for the general staff and give your tip to the lodge manager.

Tipping is less common in Botswana, Lesotho, Malawi, Mozambique, Namibia, Swaziland, Zambia, and Zimbabwe, but it is always appreciated. Loose change or 10% of fees are appropriate.

off the
beaten path

Sometimes you just need to step off the beaten path and tap into your wild side. Getting a tattoo? Need to book a stripper for a bachelor party? Whether you're hiring an escort, private dancer, or body modification artist you'll need to know how to tip these folks. In this chapter you'll read profiles of the services these professionals provide and get the lowdown on how to tip them. Before you head out to paint the town red, refer to the Off the Beaten Path Tipping Chart on pages 120 to 121.

the players

These unique services are offered in a variety of locations by uniquely talented individuals. Tipping these service providers will depend on the kind of service you're receiving and the cost of that service. Often these service providers don't expect to be tipped, but many do pay fees to their employers just to be there! Tip more when this is the case and remember that no matter what off-the-beaten-path service you choose, offering thanks through a tip is always appreciated.

TATTOO ARTIST : TIP OPTIONAL

A tattoo artist should help you choose or create a tattoo design and provide a safe, sterile, and comfortable environment. He or she should also provide you with after-care instructions and should never work while tired or under the influence of drugs and alcohol. Although gratuities are not expected by a tattoo artist, the logic for tipping this person is sound: for such a personal, not to mention permanent, service, expressing your appreciation is the right thing to do. If you opt for a predesigned tattoo, then you don't need to tip your artist unless you're really thrilled. But if an artist custom-designs a tattoo or executes one you have drawn, you should tip him or her for this added service. If you can barely afford the tattoo, don't stress about tipping. Praise and referrals are always worth more to an artist than a meager cash tip.

BODY PIERCER : TIP OPTIONAL

Good service at a piercing studio includes providing you with extensive health information: the pros and cons of a particular piercing and detailed information on post-piercing care. Tips are not expected. However, for a more complicated pierce—e.g., navel, nipple, or genital, tip your artist for the extra time it takes. If the studio is dirty or the staff is too cool for school, then take your business somewhere else. These days tattoo and body piercing studios are plentiful in most cities, so your business is more valuable than ever. Remember, you deserve attentive, friendly service from a knowledgeable, experienced staff.

"There's more reason to tip someone who creates something original and permanent on your body than someone at Denny's who, like, serves you food you're gonna forget about twenty-four hours later."
—Yetti, tattoo artist

ITTY BITTY INSIDER'S
advice

STAGE DANCER : $1–$3 PER SONG

Dancers rely heavily on tips to make their living, so tipping is an obligatory part of this form of entertainment. They must tip the doorman and the house at the end of their shift in addition to the flat fee they must pay the house. This fee ranges from $80 to $130 per shift. The amount you tip above your agreed entry fee is up to you, but whether you tip is not. How you tip will depend on how expensive the club is, who is dancing for you, and where you're seated.

Each guest is expected to give a tip for each song. If you sit at or close to the stage, you will be expected to tip on the high end. Tip less often if you sit farther away. It's standard practice to place a lump sum on the stage after a song to indicate you'd like a dancer to stop by your table.

PERFORMER WORKING THE FLOOR : $1-$5

Talking with these professionals ain't cheap. They are required to work the floor between dance sets and they certainly aren't talking to you for free. If you want attention from the performers, tip them for their time while they are at your table, or buy them a drink.

LAP DANCER : $5-$20

A lap dancer gives you one-on-one exotic attention. For this service, tip over and above the agreed-upon fee for the dance. For two or more songs in a row, tip the same amount again. Some clubs feature a private VIP room for lap dances; this service will cost more, so expect to tip more.

HIRED DANCER : 15%-20%

Going to a bachelorette party or bachelor bash? A hired dancer / stripper who comes to a hotel, restaurant, or home, arrives on time in a presentable manner, and delivers what was promised should always get a tip. Tip upon completion of the service.

ESCORT : 15%–20%

Most escort services provide nonsexual dates or companions for hire. There really isn't any tipping standard here. Tipping will depend on how much the escort service costs and how long your date lasts. Most escorts, men and women, work for agencies that require them to pay half their collected fee. They must also tip out their driver. Agencies insist that clients pay their escorts up front, in cash. A cash tip at the end of each date is expected. If your escort arrives late or is generally unpleasant to be with, don't feel obliged to tip and don't hesitate to complain to the company you booked with.

TATTOO ARTIST
TIP OPTIONAL

> *Although no tip is expected, referrals are appreciated.*
> *Tip 15% to 25% for a custom design.*

:::

BODY PIERCER
TIP OPTIONAL

> *Tip $5 to $20 for complicated or unusual piercings.*

:::

STAGE DANCER
$1–$3 PER SONG (IF SEATED AT OR NEAR THE STAGE)

> *Tip $5 to $10 if you'd like a dancer to visit your table.*

:::

PERFORMER WORKING THE FLOOR
$1–$5 FOR ATTENTION

> *Tip $3 to $5 extra if the performer arranges a lap*
> *dance for you or spends extra time chatting with you.*

:::

LAP DANCER
$5–$20

> *Tip $5 to $10 extra if the dancer cuts you a deal or*
> *spends any time talking with you.*

HIRED DANCER

15% –20%

> For special services, such as agreeing to pose for pictures with you or spending a little extra time with your group, tip $50 to $100.

:::

ESCORT

15% –20%

> Tip double for overnight or on-call service.

ITTY BITTY quick conversion chart

CHECK AMOUNT	15%	20%	CHECK AMOUNT	15%	20%
20.00	3.00	4.00	45.00	6.75	9.00
21.00	3.15	4.20	46.00	6.90	9.20
22.00	3.30	4.40	47.00	7.05	9.40
23.00	3.45	4.60	48.00	7.20	9.60
24.00	3.60	4.80	49.00	7.35	9.80
25.00	3.75	5.00	50.00	7.50	10.00
26.00	3.90	5.20	51.00	7.65	10.20
27.00	4.05	5.40	52.00	7.80	10.40
28.00	4.20	5.60	53.00	7.95	10.60
29.00	4.35	5.80	54.00	8.10	10.80
30.00	4.50	6.00	55.00	8.25	11.00
31.00	4.65	6.20	56.00	8.40	11.20
32.00	4.80	6.40	57.00	8.55	11.40
33.00	4.95	6.60	58.00	8.70	11.60
34.00	5.10	6.80	59.00	8.85	11.80
35.00	5.25	7.00	60.00	9.00	12.00
36.00	5.40	7.20	61.00	9.15	12.20
37.00	5.55	7.40	62.00	9.30	12.40
38.00	5.70	7.60	63.00	9.45	12.60
39.00	5.85	7.80	64.00	9.60	12.80
40.00	6.00	8.00	65.00	9.75	13.00
41.00	6.15	8.20	66.00	9.90	13.20
42.00	6.30	8.40	67.00	10.05	13.40
43.00	6.45	8.60	68.00	10.20	13.60
44.00	6.60	8.80	69.00	10.35	13.80

CHECK AMOUNT	15%	20%	CHECK AMOUNT	15%	20%
70.00	10.50	14.00	95.00	14.25	19.00
71.00	10.65	14.20	96.00	14.40	19.20
72.00	10.80	14.40	97.00	14.55	19.40
73.00	10.95	14.60	98.00	14.70	19.60
74.00	11.10	14.80	99.00	14.85	19.80
75.00	11.25	15.00	100.00	15.00	20.00
76.00	11.40	15.20	101.00	15.15	20.20
77.00	11.55	15.40	102.00	15.30	20.40
78.00	11.70	15.60	103.00	15.45	20.60
79.00	11.85	15.80	104.00	15.60	20.80
80.00	12.00	16.00	105.00	15.75	21.00
81.00	12.15	16.20	106.00	15.90	21.20
82.00	12.30	16.40	107.00	16.05	21.40
83.00	12.45	16.60	108.00	16.20	21.60
84.00	12.60	16.80	109.00	16.35	21.80
85.00	12.75	17.00	110.00	16.50	22.00
86.00	12.90	17.20	111.00	16.65	22.20
87.00	13.05	17.40	112.00	16.80	22.40
88.00	13.20	17.60	113.00	16.95	22.60
89.00	13.35	17.80	114.00	17.10	22.80
90.00	13.50	18.00	115.00	17.25	23.00
91.00	13.65	18.20	116.00	17.40	23.20
92.00	13.80	18.40	117.00	17.55	23.40
93.00	13.95	18.60	118.00	17.70	23.60
94.00	14.10	18.80	119.00	17.85	23.80

ITTY BITTY quick conversion chart

ITTY BITTY quick conversion chart

CHECK AMOUNT	15%	20%	CHECK AMOUNT	15%	20%
120.00	18.00	24.00	145.00	21.75	29.00
121.00	18.15	24.20	146.00	21.90	29.20
122.00	18.30	24.40	147.00	22.05	29.40
123.00	18.45	24.60	148.00	22.20	29.60
124.00	18.60	24.80	149.00	22.35	29.80
125.00	18.75	25.00	150.00	22.50	30.00
126.00	18.90	25.20	151.00	22.65	30.20
127.00	19.05	25.40	152.00	22.80	30.40
128.00	19.20	25.60	153.00	22.95	30.60
129.00	19.35	25.80	154.00	23.10	30.80
130.00	19.50	26.00	155.00	23.25	31.00
131.00	19.65	26.20	156.00	23.40	31.20
132.00	19.80	26.40	157.00	23.55	31.40
133.00	19.95	26.60	158.00	23.70	31.60
134.00	20.10	26.80	159.00	23.85	31.80
135.00	20.25	27.00	160.00	24.00	32.00
136.00	20.40	27.20	161.00	24.15	32.20
137.00	20.55	27.40	162.00	24.30	32.40
138.00	20.70	27.60	163.00	24.45	32.60
139.00	20.85	27.80	164.00	24.60	32.80
140.00	21.00	28.00	165.00	24.75	33.00
141.00	21.15	28.20	166.00	24.90	33.20
142.00	21.30	28.40	167.00	25.05	33.40
143.00	21.45	28.60	168.00	25.20	33.60
144.00	21.60	28.80	169.00	25.35	33.80

CHECK AMOUNT	15%	20%	CHECK AMOUNT	15%	20%
170.00	25.50	34.00	195.00	29.25	39.00
171.00	25.65	34.20	196.00	29.40	39.20
172.00	25.80	34.40	197.00	29.55	39.40
173.00	25.95	34.60	198.00	29.70	39.60
174.00	26.10	34.80	199.00	29.85	39.80
175.00	26.25	35.00	200.00	30.00	40.00
176.00	26.40	35.20			
177.00	26.55	35.40			
178.00	26.70	35.60			
179.00	26.85	35.80			
180.00	27.00	36.00			
181.00	27.15	36.20			
182.00	27.30	36.40			
183.00	27.45	36.60			
184.00	27.60	36.80			
185.00	27.75	37.00			
186.00	27.90	37.20			
187.00	28.05	37.40			
188.00	28.20	37.60			
189.00	28.35	37.80			
190.00	28.50	38.00			
191.00	28.65	38.20			
192.00	28.80	38.40			
193.00	28.95	38.60			
194.00	29.10	38.80			

ITTY BITTY quick conversion chart